It was Friday after school. Sam was riding
He was riding his old bike on the hill.

Just then he saw Kev. He was with his spotty mates. Kev and his spotty mates rode over to Sam.

"Hey, kid," shouted Kev. "Watch this! I bet you can't do this on your old bike!"
He rode his bike fast. Then he jumped into the air. He made his bike twist in the air.

"Cool!" said Kev's spotty mates.
"Cool!" said Sam.
"Yes!" said Kev, and he punched the air.

"I bet I can do that," said Sam. "Watch this!"
He rode his bike fast. Then he jumped into the air. He made his bike twist in the air.

The bike came down with a crash.
Sam came down with a crash.
"Oops!" said Sam.
Kev and his spotty mates laughed and laughed and laughed.

"Your bike's rubbish," sang Kev.
"Your bike's rubbish," sang his spotty mates.
"Get lost," said Sam.

Sam looked at his bike. It looked like a heap of scrap metal. The back wheel was twisted. The front wheel was twisted, too.

Sam had to push his bike home. He propped it up by the back door.

"I'll mend it in the morning," he said.

The next morning, Sam went out to mend his bike.
There was a bike propped up by the back door… but it wasn't his bike!

This bike was silver and blue – and it was brand new!
"Wow!" said Sam. "A brand new bike!"
He saw a name on the side of the bike. The name was Info-rider.

There was a small, silver box on the front of the bike. The small, silver box had a green screen. Some words flashed on the screen. "Put on the helmet," it said. "Put on the helmet."

Sam put on the helmet.
Then these words flashed on the green screen.
"Hello, Sam," said the words on the screen. "I'm Info-rider and I'm all yours!"
"Wow!" said Sam.

Just then Sam's mum came to the back door.
"Thanks, Mum," said Sam.
"Thanks for what?" said Mum.
"Thanks for my brand new bike!" said Sam.

Sam's mum looked at Info-rider.
"I didn't get you a new bike," she said. "It must be from your dad. You'll have to ask him about it."

Sam jumped on the bike and went off for a ride. He was riding along the road when…

"Look out!" flashed the screen. "Speeding car! Stop!"

Just then a car came speeding along the road.

"Thanks, Info-rider," said Sam.

Sam rode up the hill to the stream.
"I wish I could jump over the stream," he said.
"Let's jump! Let's jump!" flashed the screen.
Sam jumped right over the stream in one go.

Then the screen began to flash again.
"Look out!" it said. "Danger! Danger!"
Sam looked round.
It was Kev and his spotty mates.

"Hey, kid!" said Kev. "What's that heap of scrap metal?"
"This isn't a heap of scrap metal," said Sam. "It's my new bike. It's called Info-rider."
"Info-rider?" said Kev. "What's that?"
"Info-rider?" said Kev's spotty mates. "What's that?"

"I bet my bike can go faster than yours," said Kev.
"I bet my bike can go faster than yours!" said Sam.
"Let's have a race and see," said Kev.
"OK," said Sam. "Let's have a race."

"On your marks – get set – go!" said the spotty mates.
Kev rode very fast but Sam rode faster. Soon Sam was in front of Kev. Then…
"Look out! Danger!" flashed the screen. "Danger!"

Kev had turned his wheel. He had turned his wheel into Sam's bike.

"Let's jump! Let's jump!" flashed the screen.

Sam's bike jumped up into the air.

Kev shot under Sam. He shot under Sam… and into the stream.
"Cool!" said Kev's spotty mates.
"Yes!" said Sam.
"Oops!" said Kev.

Kev was sitting in the stream. He was wet. He was very, very wet.
"Your bike's rubbish!" sang Sam, and he punched the air.